Red Pandas

Red Pandas

Joshua Rutten

THE CHILD'S WORLD®, INC.

Library of Congress Cataloging-in-Publication Data
Rutten, Joshua.
Red pandas / by Joshua Rutten.
p.   cm.
Includes index.
Summary: Describes the physical characteristics, behavior, habitat,
and life cycle of the small, long-tailed panda of Asia.
ISBN 1-56766-473-3 (lib. bdg. : alk. paper)
1. Ailurus fulgens—Juvenile literature.
[1. Lesser pandas. 2. Pandas.]   I. Title
QL737.C214R88   1998
599.76'3—dc21   97-33250
CIP
AC

Photo Credits

ANIMALS ANIMALS © Gérard Lacz: 19
© Byron Jorjorian/Tony Stone Images: 10
© Daniel J. Cox/Natural Exposures: cover, 2, 6, 9, 15, 23, 24, 30
© 1997 Fritz Pölking/Dembinsky Photo Assoc. Inc.: 13
© John Warden/Tony Stone Images: 16
© Russ Kinne/Comstock, Inc.: 20, 26, 29

On the cover...

Front cover: This red panda is watching other forest animals.
Page 2: This red panda is resting in a tree.

Table of Contents

Deep in the Asian forest, the night air is cool and damp. Many animals are asleep, and the forest is quiet. Suddenly, there is a movement in the trees. A white face appears and looks around. Slowly the animal climbs down from the trees and begins looking for roots and berries to eat. What type of creature is this? It's a red panda!

Are All Pandas Related?

Red pandas belong to a group of animals called **mammals**. A mammal is an animal with hair all over its body. Mammal mothers feed their babies with milk from their bodies. Dogs, horses, and people are mammals, too.

Most people think that all pandas are big, black-and-white animals. But only the *giant panda* looks like that. Giant pandas live in the mountains of China. They can grow to be over 300 pounds. But red pandas weigh only about 10 pounds. They look more like raccoons than bears.

It is easy to see why many people mistake red pandas for raccoons. ⇒

What Do Red Pandas Look Like?

Red pandas have small bodies and strong legs. They also have sharp claws for climbing and grabbing. Red pandas have a white face, a black nose, and ears that stick straight up. They also have a long, striped tail. But the most beautiful thing about red pandas is their thick orange fur. It is often soft and shiny.

⇐ This red panda is using its claws to hold on to a branch.

Where Do Red Pandas Live?

Most animals live only in one type of place. This is the animal's **environment**. If an animal's environment is destroyed, the animal will die. The red panda lives only in the mountain forests of certain countries in Asia. If these forests are destroyed, the red panda will die out.

The red panda spends most of its life in the trees. There it is safe and happy. Red pandas even have their babies in trees!

This red panda is resting in the early morning sunshine. ⇒

Red pandas are **nocturnal** animals. That means they sleep during the day and are active at night. When darkness falls in the forest, the red panda wakes up. It climbs down from the treetops to look for food. The cool night hours are perfect for exploring and eating. All night long, the red panda walks and plays. When the sun begins to rise, the red panda goes back to its tree. There it snuggles down and falls asleep for the day.

As the sun sets, this red panda begins to look for food. ⇒

To get the energy it needs, the red panda spends most of its time eating. It eats the large leaves of the *bamboo* plant. But sometimes it cannot find enough bamboo to eat. Then the red panda looks for other things to eat. Fruit, berries, insects, and mice are all favorite foods. Since red pandas eat both plants and other animals, they are called **omnivores**. People and raccoons are omnivores, too.

Bamboo leaves are very big. They are so big that red pandas sometimes have trouble eating them. To help hold on to their food, red pandas have a special bone near their wrists. This bone acts like a thumb. This "thumb" helps the red panda grab its food and hold it tightly.

⇐ This red panda is eating a large bamboo leaf.

How Are Baby Red Pandas Born?

Red pandas like to live alone. The only time the male and female red pandas get together is when they mate. Four months later, the female finds a hollow tree. She makes a warm bed of leaves and sticks inside the tree. There she gives birth to between one and four **cubs**, or babies. When the cubs are born, they weigh less than half a pound. They can't even see until they are 20 days old!

This older red panda cub is calling for its mother. ⇒

The mother red panda takes very good care of her cubs. When they are very small, she feeds them milk from her body. As they get older, she teaches them how to find food and hunt small animals. She even teaches them how to stay safe in the forest. After about a year, the cubs leave their mother and go off on their own.

Do Red Pandas Have Any Enemies?

Red pandas live high in the trees, out of reach of most enemies. And very few animals hunt at night, when the red pandas are active. But sometimes a wild dog or leopard finds a red panda on the ground. If the red panda cannot get to a tree quickly, the dog or leopard may eat it.

This red panda is climbing quickly to safety. ⇒

The red pandas' biggest enemy, though, is people. When people move into the mountains, they destroy the red pandas' environment. They cut down the bamboo plants that the pandas eat. They also cut down the trees in which the pandas live. Without their environment, red pandas may soon die out. They are called **endangered** animals because there are so few left in the wild.

⇐ This red panda is stretched out on a high branch.

Endangered animals are often protected by laws. But sometimes people ignore the laws. When people kill animals that are protected, they are called **poachers**. Some poachers hunt red pandas. So even though red pandas are protected by laws, they are still not safe.

What Can Be Done To Save Red Pandas?

With so few red pandas left, scientists are trying very hard to save them. Most of the countries where the red pandas live have created parks to protect the red pandas' environment. Many zoos around the world are trying to raise red pandas and their cubs. They hope someday to return some red pandas to the wild.

This red panda lives in a zoo where it is safe. ⇒

We are lucky to be living in a time when there are still red pandas. These gentle, quiet creatures are fun to watch and learn about. But if we do not work to save them, these strange and beautiful animals will be gone forever. So the next time you wonder about how to make the world a better place, think about the red panda. Maybe YOU can think of a few ways to help them, too!

⇐ This red panda has beautiful, shiny fur.

Glossary

cubs (KUBZ)
A baby red panda is called a cub. Red panda cubs stay with their mother for about a year.

endangered (en–DANE–jerd)
When an animal is endangered, it is in danger of dying out. Red pandas are endangered animals.

environment (en–VY–run–ment)
An animal's environment is the area in which it lives. The red panda's environment is the cold mountain forests of Asia.

mammals (MA–mullz)
Mammals are animals that have hair and feed their babies milk from their bodies. Red pandas, dogs, horses, and people are all mammals.

nocturnal (nok–TUR–null)
Nocturnal animals are active only at night. Red pandas are mostly nocturnal.

omnivore (OM–ni–vor)
An omnivore is an animal that eats both plants and other animals. Red pandas are omnivores.

poachers (POH–cherz)
Poachers are people that kill animals illegally. Some poachers hunt red pandas.

Index